GREATEST HITS

CONTENTS

Produced by
Alfred Music
P.O. Box 10003
Van Nuys, CA 91410-0003
alfred.com

Printed in USA.

ISBN-10: 1-4706-1703-X
ISBN-13: 978-1-4706-1703-5

BREAK ON THROUGH

(To the Other Side)

Words and Music by
THE DOORS

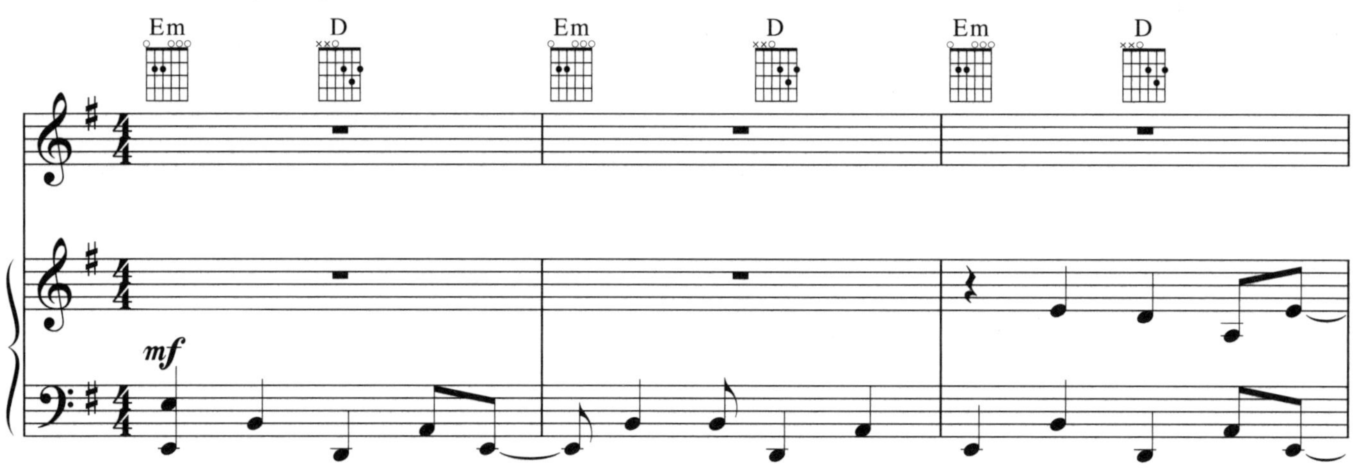

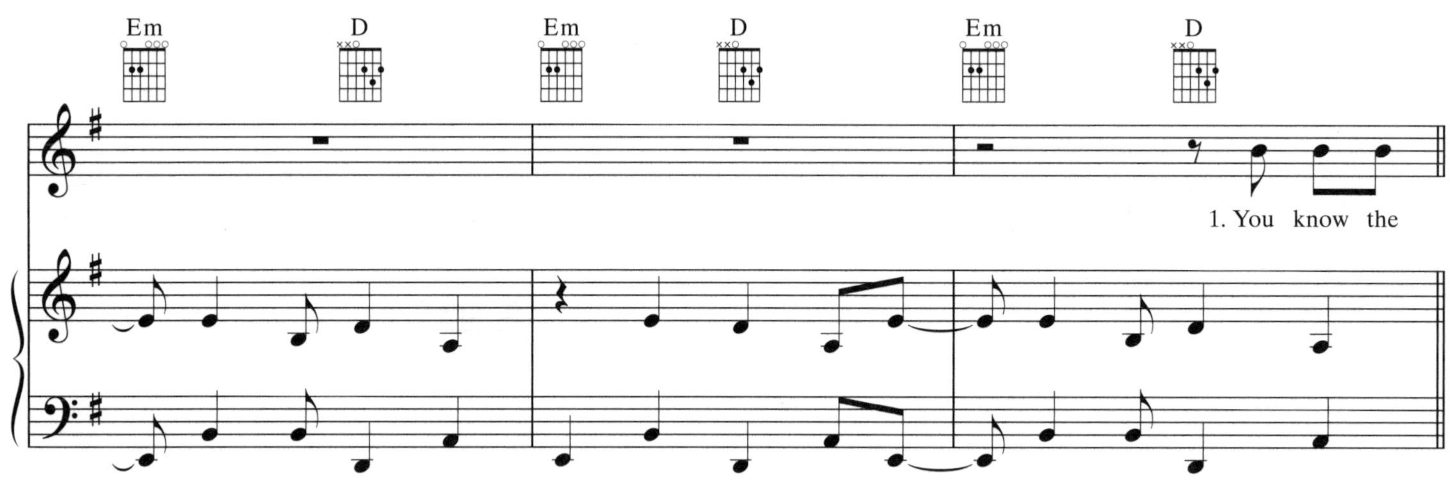

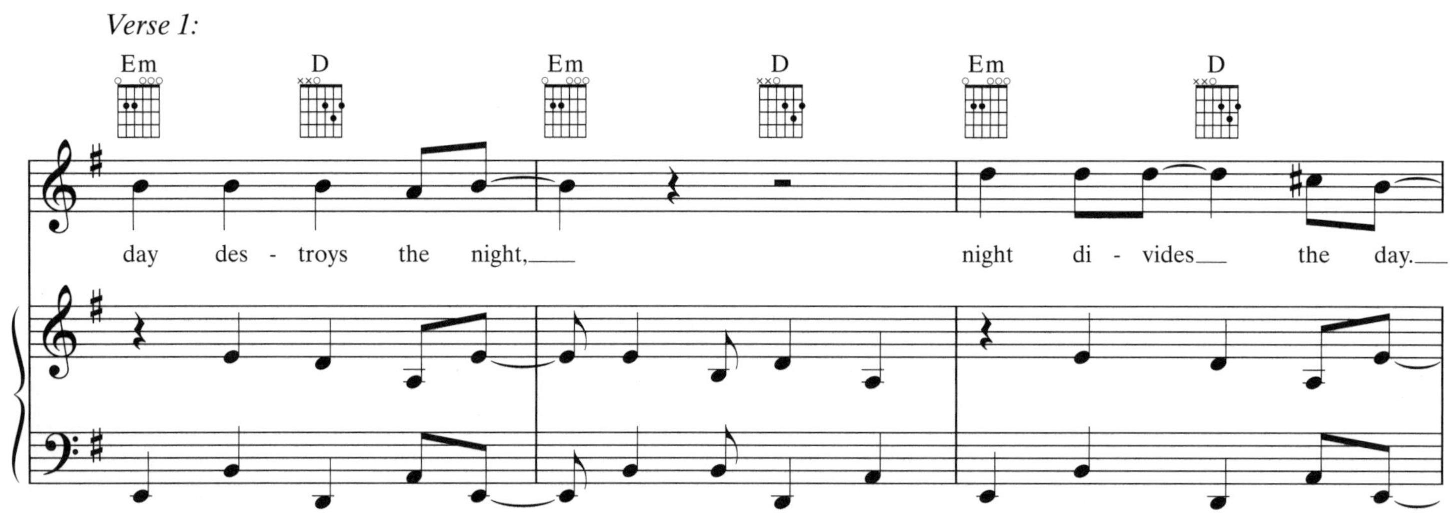

Em
D
Tried to run,
tried to hide...
Em
Break on through to the oth - er side.
Break on through to the
oth - er side.
Break on through to the oth - er side, yeah.
Em
D
Em
D
Em
D
Em
D
2. We

Verse 2:
Em
D
Em
D
Em
D
chased our pleas - ures here,
dug our treas - ures there.
Em
D
But can you still re - call the time we cried?
Em
Break on through to the oth - er side.
Break on through to the
oth - er side.

Organ solo:
Em
D
Em
D
Em
D
Em
D
Ev - 'ry - bod - y___ loves my ba - by.___

Em
D
Ev - 'ry - bod - y
loves my ba - by.
She gets,
she gets,
she gets,
she gets,
yeah.
3. I found an

Verse 3:
Em
D
Em
D
Em
D
is - land in your arms, a coun - try in your eyes.
Em
D
Arms that chain us, eyes that lied.
Em
Break on through to the oth - er side.
Break on through to the
oth - er side.
Break on through, ow!
Oh,

E7(♯9)
6
yeah!
Verse 4:
4. Made the scene, from week to week, day to day,
D
hour to hour. Gate is straight, deep and wide...

Em
Break on through to the oth - er side.
Break on through to the oth - er side.
Break on through.
Break on through.
Break on through.
Break on through.
Yeah, yeah, yeah, yeah,
yeah, yeah, yeah, yeah, yeah.

THE END

Gtr. in Dbl. Drop D tuning:
⑥ = D ③ = G
⑤ = A ② = B
④ = D ① = D

Words and Music by
THE DOORS

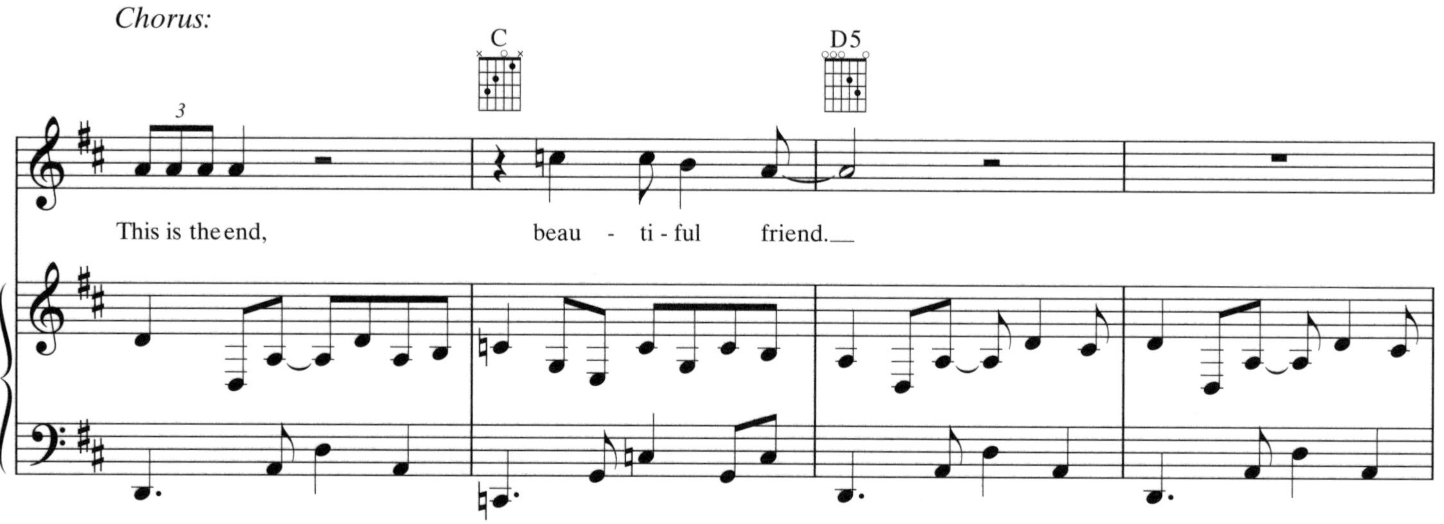

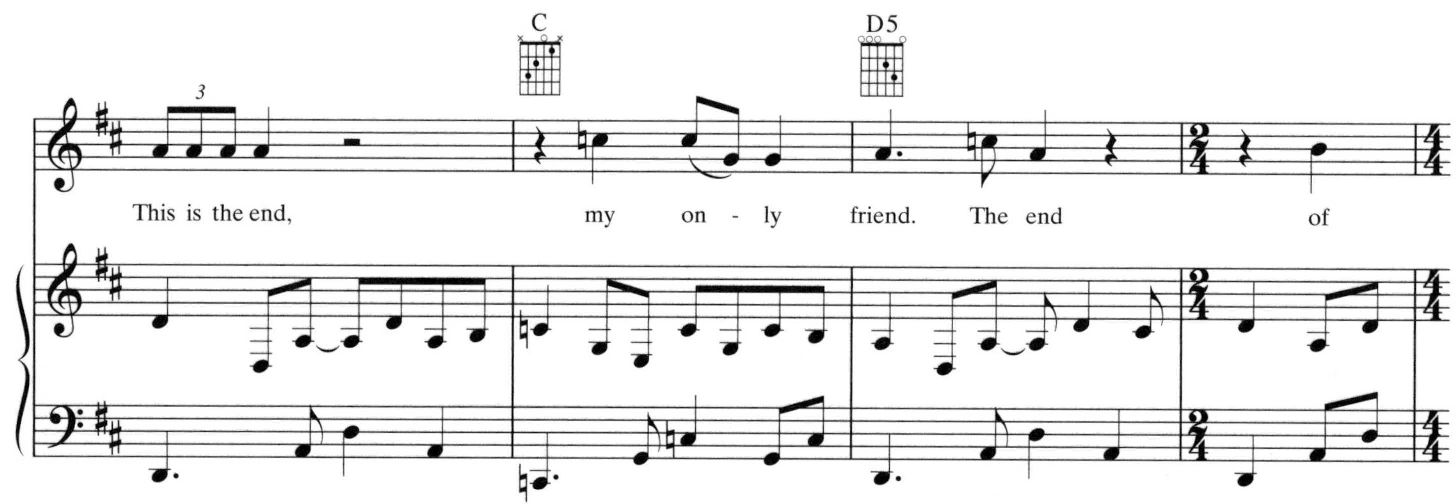

C
G
D5
our e - lab - 'rate plans. The end of ev - 'ry - thing_ that
stands, the end. No safe - ty or___ sur -
prise, the end. I'll nev - er look in - to your
eyes a - gain.___ Can you

Bridge:
C
D5
G
D5
pic - ture what will be, so___ lim - it - less and__ free.
C
D5
G
Des - p'rate - ly____ in need__ of some stran - ger's hand__
D5
C
D5
__ in a... des - p'rate__ land.

1.2.3.
Instrumental:
(Guitar solo ad lib.)
4.
Verse 1:
1. Lost in a Ro-man wil-der-ness of pain.
And all the chil-dren are in-

sane.
All the
chil-dren
are in - sane.
Wait - ing for the
sum-mer rain,
yeah.

2. There's
Verses 2, 3 & 4:
dan-ger on the edge of town.
3.4. See additional lyrics
Ride the king's high - way, ba - by.
Weird scenes in - side the gold mine.

Ride the high - way west, ba - by.
Ride the snake, ride the snake
to the lake. the an - cient lake, ba - by.
The snake, he's long, sev - en miles.

1.
Ride the snake...
He's old,
and his skin is cold.
2.
3. The
(Spoken:) 4. The
3.
Moth-er,

I want to...
love you, yeah.
Come on, yeah!
f
mp

Verse 5:

5. C'-mon, ba-by, take a chance with us.
cresc. poco a poco
C'-mon, ba-by, take a chance with us.
C'-mon, ba-by, take a chance with us and meet me at the back of the blue bus, do-in' a
blue rock all night, blue bus, do-in' a blue rock. Come on, yeah!
accel.

Faster ♩ = 124

Instrumental:

Repeat as desired for solo

Freely

Tempo I (♩ = 112)
1.
2.
mp
Chorus:
C
D5
This is the end, beau - ti - ful friend.
C
D5
This is the end, my on - ly friend, the end. It hurts to
set you free, but you'll nev-er fol-low me.

Verse 3:
The West is the best.
The West is the best.
Get here and we'll do the rest.
The blue bus is callin' us.
The blue bus is callin' us.
Driver, where you takin' us?

Verse 4:
Spoken:
The killer awoke before dawn, he put his boots on.
He took a face from the ancient gallery and he walked on down the hall.
He went into the room where his sister lived, and... then he paid a visit to his brother,
And then he... he walked on down the hall, yeah, and he came to a door... and he looked inside.
"Father," "Yes, son," "I want to kill you."
Mother, I want to... love you, yeah. Come on, yeah!

THE GHOST SONG

Words and Music by
THE DOORS

Moderately ♩ = 120

With a funky groove
Em7
A/E
A vast radiant beach and cooled jeweled moon.
mf
Em7
A/E
Couples naked race down by it's quiet side and we laugh like soft, mad children,
Em7
A6/E
Em
A6/E
Em
A6/E
smug in the wooly cotton brains of infancy, the music and voices are all around us.
Em7
A6/E
Em7
A6/E
Em7
A/E
A6/E
Em7

Em7
A/E
Choose they croon the Ancient Ones, the time has come again choose now, they croon, beneath the moon beside an ancient lake.
Em7
A/E
Enter again the sweet forest, enter the hot dream. Come with us, everything is broken up and dances.
Em7
(Keyboard solo)

N.C.
Indians scattered, on dawn's highway bleeding, ghosts crowd the young child's fragile eggshell mind.

Gm7 C/G Gm11 Gm7

We have assembled inside,

C/G Gm11 Gm7 C/G Gm11

this ancient and insane theater to propagate our lust for life, and flee the swarming wisdom of the streets.

Gm7

The barns have stormed, the windows kept,

(Guitar solo)

and only one of all the rest, to dance and save us from the divine mockery of words, music inflames temperament.

Gm9
Gm11
Gm9
Gm11
Gm9
Gm11
Gm9
Gm11
Gm9
Gm11
Gm9
Gm11
Gm9
Oh great creator of being,
grant us one more hour, to perform our art and perfect our lives.
We need great golden copulations....

Gm11
Gm9
Gm11
Gm9
Gm11
Gm9
Gm11
When the true king's murderer's are allowed to roam free, a thousand magicians arise in the land.
Gm7
N.C.
Where are the feasts we were promised?
15ma

HELLO, I LOVE YOU

Words and Music by
THE DOORS

A5
N.C.
A
G
jump in your game.
Hel - lo,
I love you, won't you
A5
N.C.
A
G
tell me your name?
Hel - lo,
I love you, let me
Verse 1:
A5
N.C.
A
G
A
G
jump in your game.
1. She's walk - ing down the street,
A
G
A
G
A
G
blind to ev - 'ry eye she meets.
Do you think you'll be the

A
G
A
G
A
G
guy to make the queen of the an-gels sigh? Hel-
Chorus:
A
G
A5
N.C.
lo, I love you, won't you tell me your name? Hel-
A
G
A5
N.C.
lo, I love you, let me jump in your game. Hel-
A
G
A5
N.C.
lo, I love you, won't you tell me your name? Hel-

A G A5 N.C.

lo, I love you, let me jump in your game.___ 2. She

Verse 2:

A G A G A G

holds her__ head so high;___ like a stat - ue__ in the

A G A G A G

sky.___ Her arms are__ wick - ed and her legs are long.__ When she

A G A G

moves my brain screams out this song.___

A
A
D
Glissando
Glissando
Glissando
Verse 3:
B♭
A♭
3. Side - walk crouch - es at her feet, like a dog that begs for
some-thing sweet. Do you hope to make her see, you fool? Do you
hope to pluck this dusk-y jew - el? Hel - lo! Hel - lo!

B♭
A♭
Hel - lo!
Hel - lo!
Hel - lo!
Hel-lo!
Hel - lo!
I want
(Hel - lo!)
you.
(Hel - lo!)
I need
(Hel - lo!)
Repeat ad lib. and fade
my
babe,
hel - lo.
(Hel - lo!)
(Hel - lo!)

L.A. WOMAN

Words and Music by
THE DOORS

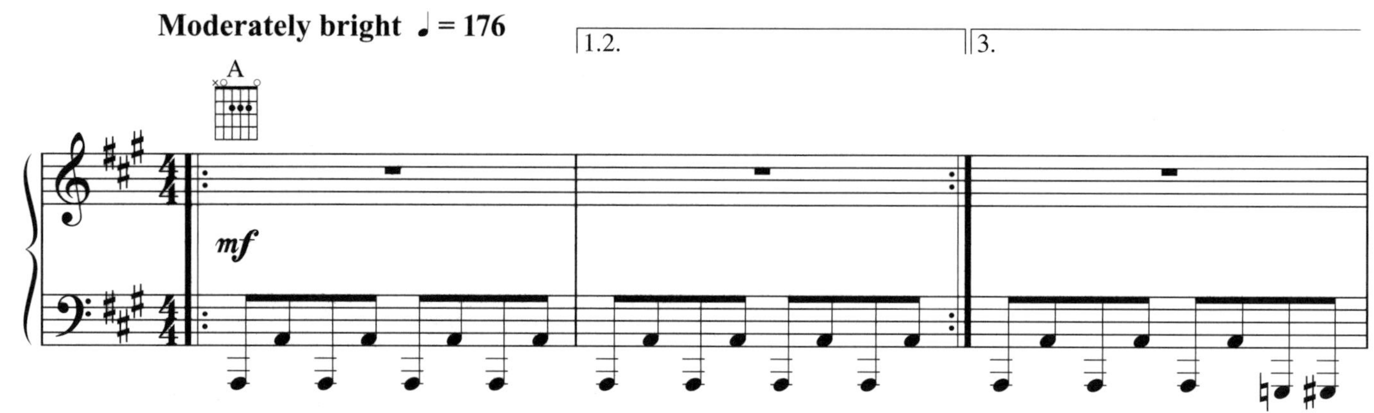

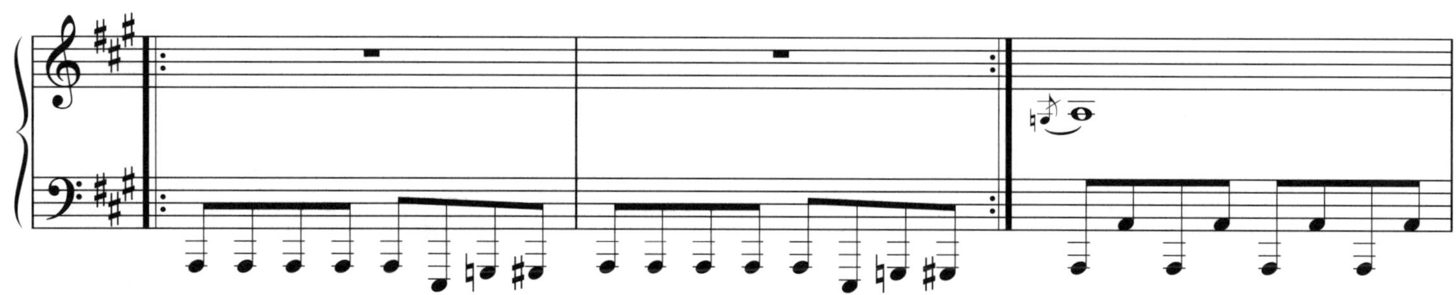

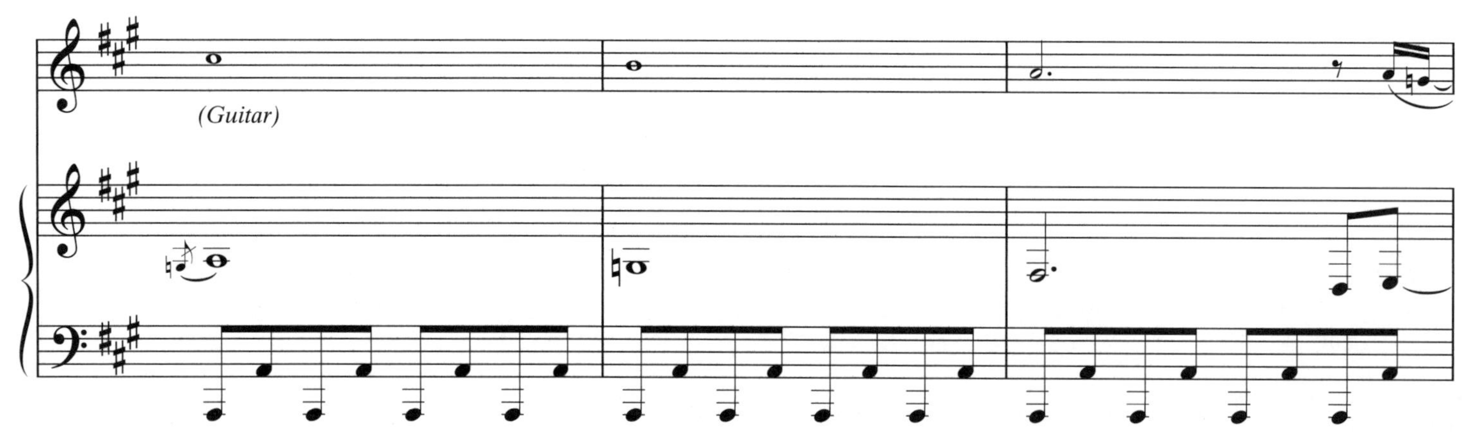

1. Well, I
Verse 1:
just got in - to town a - bout an hour a - go.
(Guitar)
8vb
I took a look a-round, see which way the wind blows.
8vb
With a lit - tle girl in a

Hol - ly - wood bun - ga - low.
Are you a
luck - y lit - tle la - dy in the cit - y of light?
Or just an - oth - er lost an - gel?
Cit - y of night,
cit - y of night.
G
3
A
5

G
City of night,
city of night.
A
Whoa! Come on!
Guitar solo:
(Inst. solo ad lib.…

...end solo)

Chorus:

L. A.__ wom - an,
L. A.__ wom - an.

L. A. wom - an, Sun-day af - ter - noon.__

L. A. wom - an, Sun - day
af - ter - noon.
L. A. wom - an, Sun - day af - ter - noon,
drive through your sub - urbs
G
3
in - to your blues.
In - to your

A
G
blues, yeah! In - to your blue, blue, blue,
A
in - to your blues. Oh,
Piano solo:
yeah.

Interlude 1:
A
5
G
3
A
5
G
3
(Piano 2)
A
5
G
3
1.
A
5
G
3
2.
A
5
G
3
I

Bridge 1:

A G A G A G

see your hair is burn - ing;

A G A G A G

hills are filled with fire.

A G A G A G

If they say I nev - er

A G A G A G

loved you, you

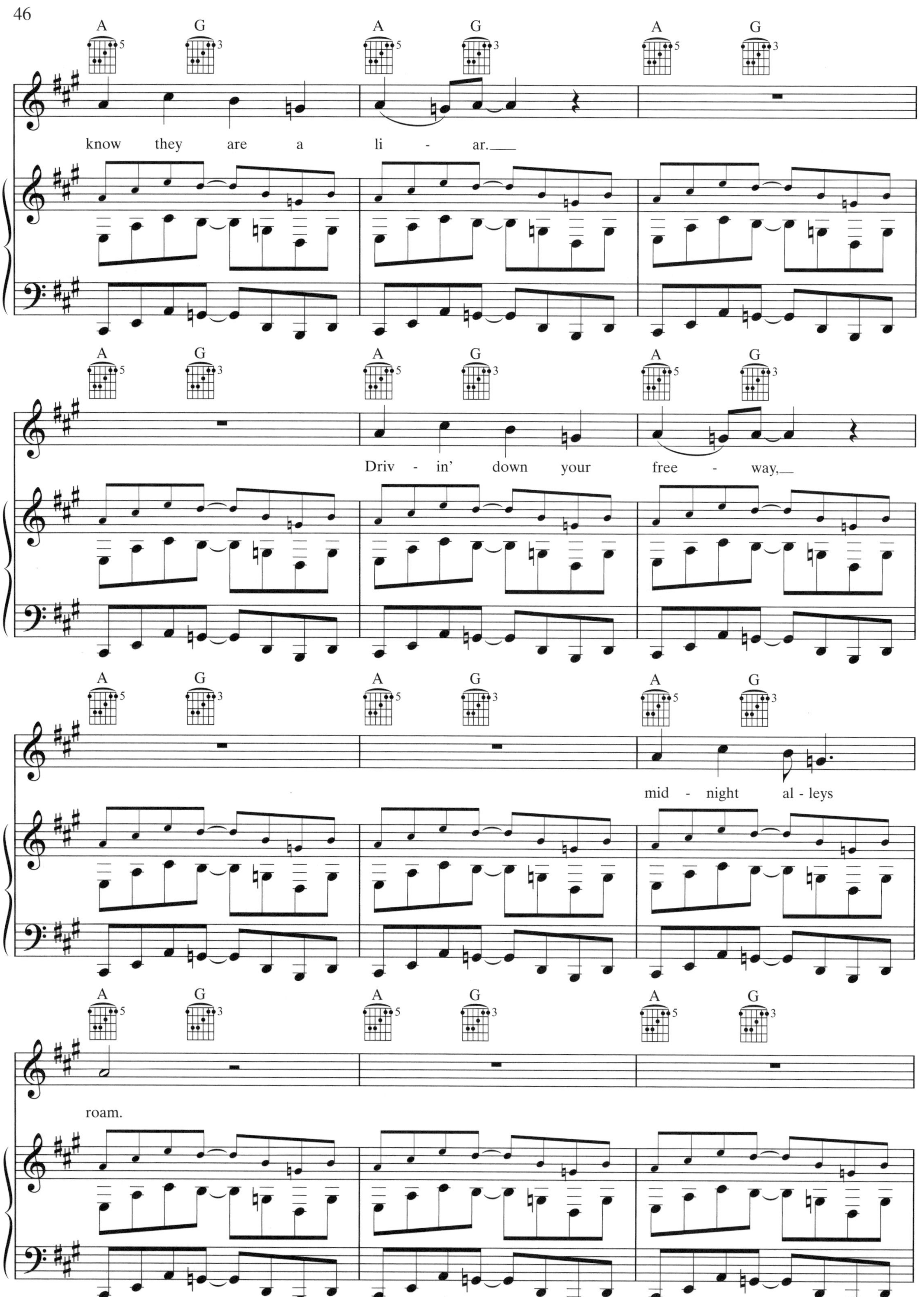

A
G
know they are a li - ar.
Driv - in' down your free - way,
mid - night al - leys
roam.

A
Cops in cars, the top - less bars,
nev - er saw a wom - an
so a - lone,
G
so a - lone,
A
So a -
G
lone,
so a - lone.
A

Mo - tel mon - ey, mur - der mad - ness,
a - change the mood from glad_
__ to sad - ness.
Half time ♩ = 88
Am7
mp
decel. poco a poco

1.2. | 3.

Slowly ♩ = 72

Bridge 2:

A5 C5 A5 A5 C5 A5

Mis - ter Mo - jo ris - in'. Mis - ter Mo - jo ris - in'. Mis - ter

mf

accel. poco a poco

A5 C5 A5 A5 C5 A5

Mo - jo ris - in'.______ Mis - ter Mo - jo ris - in'.______

A5 C5 A5

Got - ta keep on ris - in'.______ Mis - ter

continue accel. poco a poco

A5
C5
A5
A5
C5
A5
Mo - jo ris - in'.
Mis - ter Mo - jo ris - in'.
A5
C5
A5
Mo - jo ris - in'.
Got my
A5
C5
A5
A5
C5
A5
Mo - jo ris - in'.
Mis - ter Mo - jo ris - in'.
A5
C5
A5
Got - ta keep on ris - in'.

A5
C5
A5
Right in, right in.
Go - in' right in, right in.
continue accel. poco a poco
Go - in' right in, right in.
I got - ta
ride in, ride in.
Babe, right in, right in.
Tempo I (♩ = 176)
C
I got - ta whoa! Yeah. Right.

D
10
Oh,
yeah.
A
5
Verse 2:
2. Well,
just got in - to town a - bout an hour a - go.

Took a look a - round me, which
way the wind_ blows.
With a lit - tle girl in a Hol - ly - wood bun - ga - low.___
Are you a luck - y lit - tle la - dy in the cit - y of light?__

Or just an - oth - er lost an - gel?
City - y of night.
G
3
A
5
Cit - y of night.
Cit - y of night.
G
3
A
5
Cit - y of night.
Whoa!

Guitar solo:
Come on!
(Inst. solo ad lib....
Chorus:
Repeat ad lib. and fade
L. A. Wom - an.
L. A. Wom - an.

LIGHT MY FIRE

Words and Music by
THE DOORS

Am7
F♯m7
Am7
if I was to say to you,
girl, we could-n't get much high -
Try now, we can on - ly lose,
and our love be-come a fu - n'ral pyre.
F♯m7
Chorus:
G
A
D
er.
Come on, ba - by, light my fire.
mf
G
A
D
B
G
D
Come on, ba - by, light my fire.
Try to set the night on
1.
E
2.
E
fi - re.
2.The
fi - re!
Yeah.

Am7
Bm7
Organ solo:

Am7
Bm7
8va

Am7
Bm7
(8va)

Am7
Bm7
Guitar solo...
1.-7.
8.

Am7
Bm7
Am7
Bm7
Am7
Bm7
Am7
Bm7
Am7
Bm7
G
D
F
B♭
f
E♭
A♭
A
3. The
Verse 3:
Am7
F♯m7
Am7
time to hes - i - tate is through.
No time to wal - low in the mire.
mp

F♯m7
Am7
F♯m7
Try now we can on - ly lose
and our
Chorus:
Am7
F♯m7
G
A
love be - come a fu - n'ral pyre.
Come on, ba - by, light my fire.
D
G
A
D
B
Come on, ba - by, light my fire.
G
D
E
Try to set the night on fi - re!
Yeah.
4. You

Verse 4:
Am7
F♯m7
Am7
know that it would be un - true,
you know that I would be a liar
mf
F♯m7
Am7
F♯m7
if I was to say to you,
Am7
F♯m7
girl, we could - n't get much high - er.
Chorus:
G
A
D
G
A
Come on, ba - by, light my fire.
Come on, ba - by, light my fi -
f

D F C D

re. Try to set the night on fi - re.

F C D F C

Try to set the night on fi - re. Try to set the night on fi -

D F C D

re.___ Try to set the night on fi - re!___

G D F B♭ E♭ A♭ A

4

LOVE HER MADLY

Words and Music by
THE DOORS

Moderately fast ♩ = 144

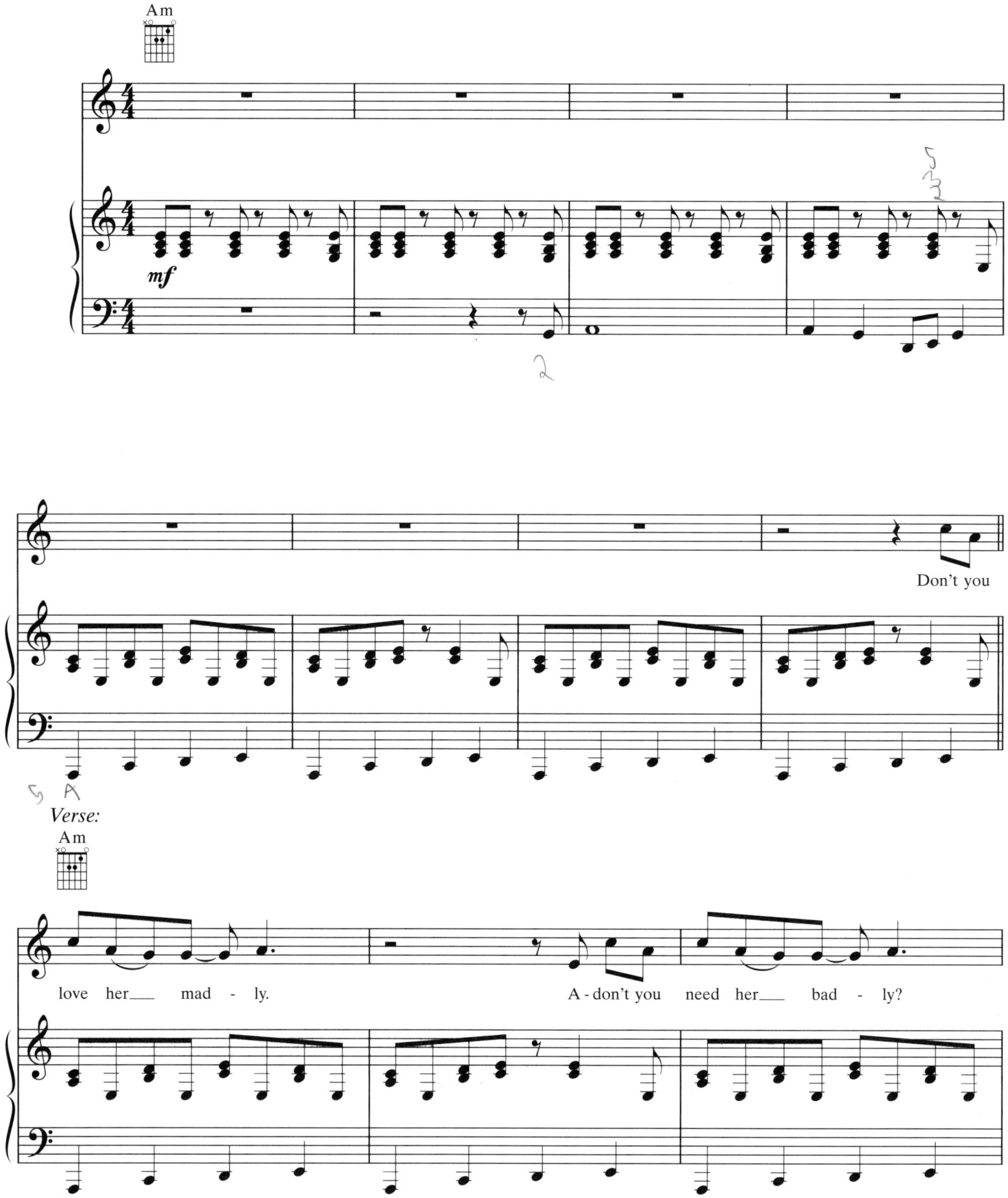

Don't you

Verse:

Am

love her___ mad - ly. A - don't you need her___ bad - ly?

D
Don't you love her ways?
A - tell me
Am
what you say.
A - don't you love her mad - ly?
C
F
D
Wan - na be her dad - dy?
A - don't you
Am
love her face?
Don't you love her as she's

E
Am
walk - ing out the door,
like she did one thous - and times be - fore?
E
Am
D
Don't you love her ways?
A - tell me
Am
what you say.
Don't you love her as she's

E
Am
E
Am
walk - ing out the door?
Bridge:
D
All your love,
all your love,
all your love,
all your love...
All your love is gone,
G

C
so sing a lone - ly song
of a
A
D
deep blue dream.
Sev - en hors - es seem
To Coda
F
D
G
E
Am
to be on the mark.
Organ solo:

C
Yeah, don't you
F
D
Am
love her? Don't you love her as she's
E
Am
E
Am
D.S. 𝄋 al Coda
walk - ing out the door?

Coda
Am
mark.
(Guitar)
Instrumental solo:
Dm
Am
C
F

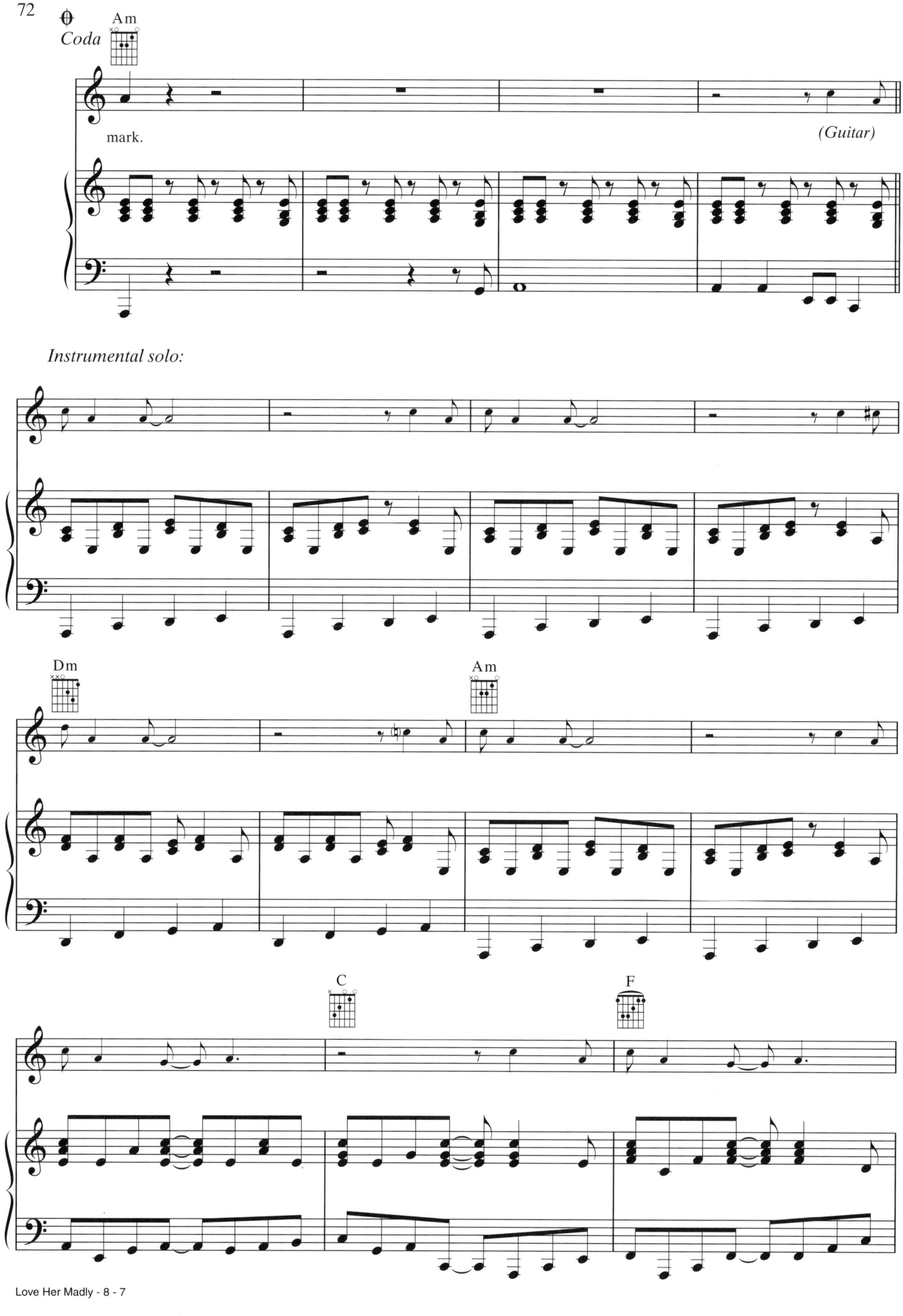

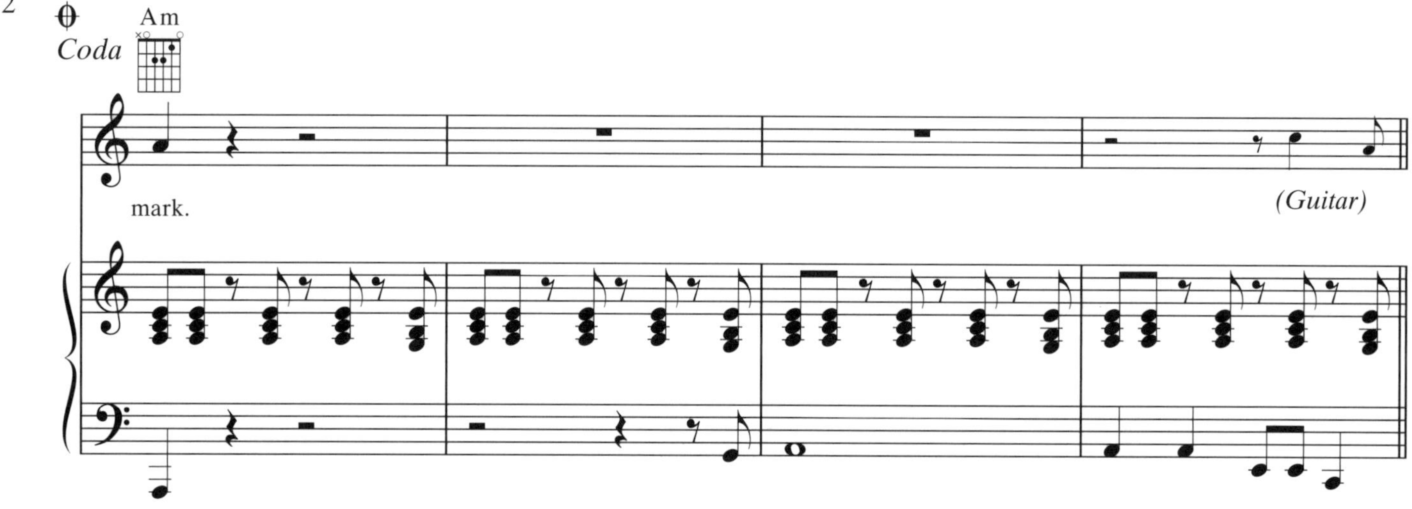

D
Am
Well, don't you love her mad - ly?
Ah, don't you love her mad - ly?
Ah, don't you love her mad - ly?
Repeat ad lib. and fade

PEOPLE ARE STRANGE

Words and Music by
THE DOORS

Chorus:
B7
G
B
strange,
fac - es come out of the rain,
when you're strange.
B7
G
B
No one re - mem - bers your name,
when you're strange,
B7
when you're strange,
when you're
strange.
Verse 2:
Em
Am
Em
Am
Em
2. Peo - ple are strange,
when you're a stran - ger,
fac - es look ug - ly

B7
Em
Am
Em
when you're a - lone.
Wom-en seem wick - ed
when you're un - want - ed,
Am
Em
B7
Em
B
streets are un - e - ven
when you're down.
(Guitar solo ad lib....
Em
B
Em
...end solo)
When you're

Chorus:
B7
G
B
strange,
fac - es come out
of the rain,
when you're strange.
B7
G
B
No one re - mem - bers your name,
when you're strange,
B7
when you're strange,
when you're
strange.
Al - right,
yeah.

Em
Am
Em
Am
Em
B7
Em
Am
Em
Am
Em
B7
Em
When you're
Chorus:
B7
G
strange,
fac - es come out of the rain,

B7
when you're strange.
G
B7
No one re - mem - bers your name,
when you're strange,
when you're strange,
when you're
strange.

RIDERS ON THE STORM

Words and Music by
THE DOORS

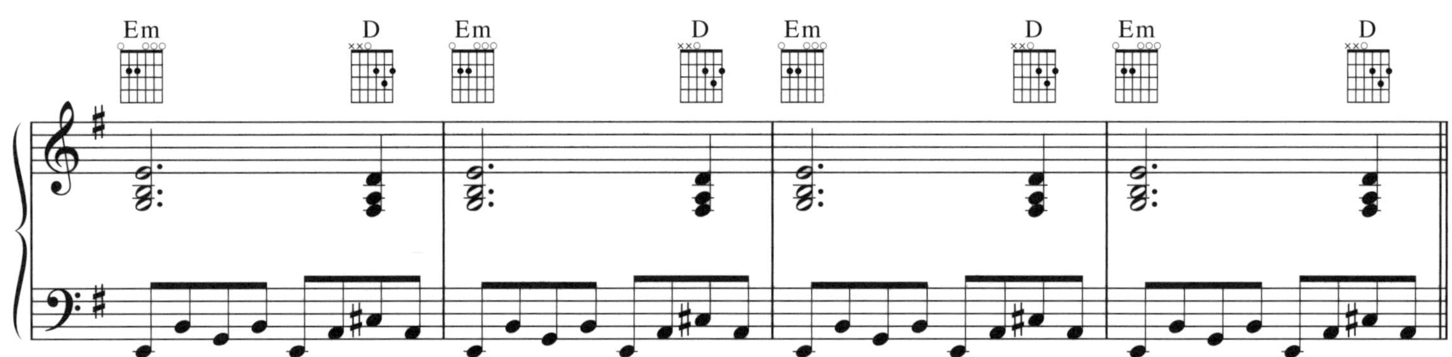

Verse 1:

Em D Em D Em D

1. Rid - ers on the storm, rid - ers on the storm.

Em Am Bm/A Am7 D/A

In - to this house we're born, in -

Em D Em G/D D

to this world we're thrown. Like a dog with - out a bone, an

C Em A Em7 A

act - or out on loan. Rid - ers on the storm. 2. There's a

Verse 2:
Em
A
Em7
A
Em
A
kill - er on the road;
his brain is squirm - ing like a toad.
sim.
Em7
A
Am
Bm/A
Am7
D/A
Take a long hol - i - day;
Em
D
Em
G/D
D
let your chil - dren play.
If you give this man a ride, sweet
C
Em
A
Em7
A
fam - i - ly will die.
Kill - er on the road.
Yeah.

Guitar solo:
Em
8vb
mf
Am
Bm/A
Am7
D/A
Em
(8vb)
Em
G/D
D
C
Em
A
(8vb)
Em7
A
Em
A
Em7
A
(8vb)
3. Girl, you

Verse 3:
Em A Em7 A Em A
got - ta love your man. Girl, you got - ta love your man.
sim.
Em7 A Am Bm/A Am7 D/A
Take him by the hand;
Em D Em G/D D
make him un - der - stand. The world on you de - pends, our
C Em A Em7 A
life will nev - er end. Got - ta love your man. Yeah.

Electric piano solo:

Em A Em A Em A

Em A Em A Em A

Em A Em A Em A

Em A Em A Em A

Em A Em A Em A

3

Em
A
Em
A
Em
A
Em
A
Em
A
Em
A
Em
A
Em
A
Em
A
Em
A
Em
A
Em
A
Em
A
Em
A
Em
A
3

Em
A
cresc.
f
mf
8va

Em
A
Em
A
Em
D
mp
Em
D
Em
D
Em
p
Em
A
Em7
A
Em
A
mp
Em7
A
Em
A
Em7
A
Em
A
Em7
A

Verse 4:

Em A Em7 A Em A

4. Rid - ers on the storm, rid - ers on the storm.

sim.

Em7 A Am Bm/A Am7 D/A

In - to this house we're born, in -

Em D Em G/D D

to this world we're thrown. Like a dog with - out a bone, an

C Em A Em7 A

act - or out on loan. Rid - ers on the storm.

Em
A
Rid - ers on the storm._
Rid - ers on the storm._

Em
A
8va
freely
(8va)
l.h. decresc.
Rubato
Em7
p

LOVE ME TWO TIMES

Words and Music by
THE DOORS

Moderately ♩ = 126 (♫ = ♩♪ triplet)

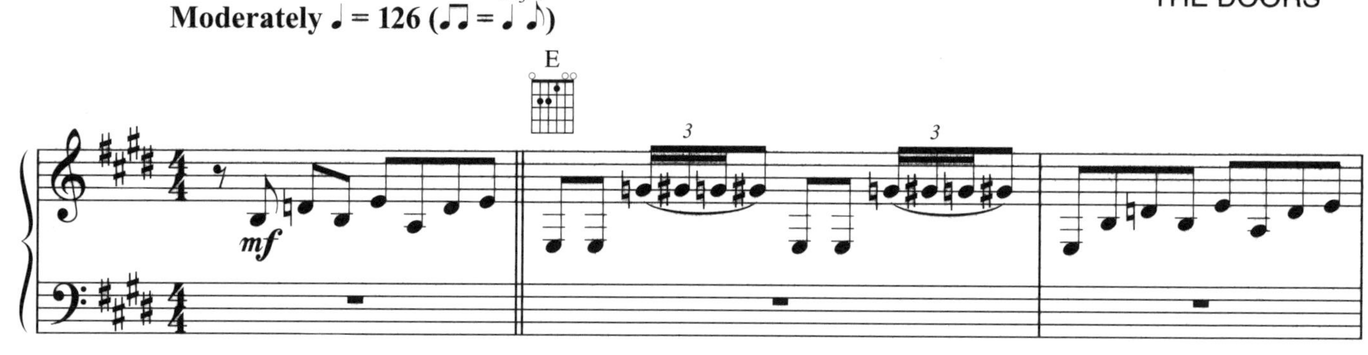

Verse 1:

A7
Love me two times, girl, I'm go - in' a - way.
E
D
Love me two times, girl,
C7(♯9)
one for to - mor - row, one just for to - day.
G
D
C7
B7
E
Love me two times, I'm go - in' a - way.

Verse 2:
2. Love me one time,
I could not speak.
Love me one time,
A7
E
yeah, my knees gone weak.
Love me two times, girl,

D
lasts me, all through the week.
C7(♯9)
G
D
C7
B7
Love me two times, I'm go - in' a - way.
E7(♯9)
G
D
Love me two times,
C7
B7
E
I'm go - in' a - way.
Al - right, yeah!

Keyboard solo:
E
A7
E
G
D
C7
B7
E7(♯9)
G
D
C7
B7
E

3. Love me one time,
Verse 3:
I could not speak.
A7
Love me one time, ba - by,

E
yeah, my knees_ gone weak._
Love me two times,_ girl,_
D
last me, all through the week._
C7(♯9)
G
D
C7
B7
Love me two times,_ I'm go - in' a - way._
(3)
E
Verse 4:
4. Love me two times, babe,___

love me twice to - day.
Love me two times, babe,
A7
E
'cause I'm go - in' a - way.
D
Love me two times, girl,
one for to - mor - row,
C7(♯9)
G
D
one just for to - day.
Love me two times,
3
3
3
3

C7
B7
E7(♯9)
I'm go - in' a - way.
G
D
C7
B7
E7(♯9)
Love me two times,
I'm go - in' a - way.
G
D
Love me two times,
I'm
C7
B7
E7(♯9)
go - in' a - way.

ROADHOUSE BLUES

Words and Music by
THE DOORS

1. A-keep your
Verse 1:
eyes on the road, your hands upon the wheel.
Keep your eyes on the road, your hands upon the wheel.
Yeah, we're goin' to the road - house,

gon - na have a real old,
a good time.
Verse 2:
2. Yeah, in back of the road - house they got some bun - ga-lows.
Yeah, in back of the road - house, they

got some_ bun - ga - lows.___ And
that's for the peo-ple who like to go___ down slow.___
Chorus:
A7
Let it roll,___ ba - by, roll.___ Let it
roll,___ ba - by, roll.___ Let it roll,___ ba - by, roll._
8va

B7
C7
B7
Let it roll
all night
(8va)
E7
long.
Guitar solo ad lib. under piano figure…

8va
(8va)
(8va)
You got - ta
dim. ...end solo)

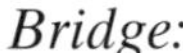

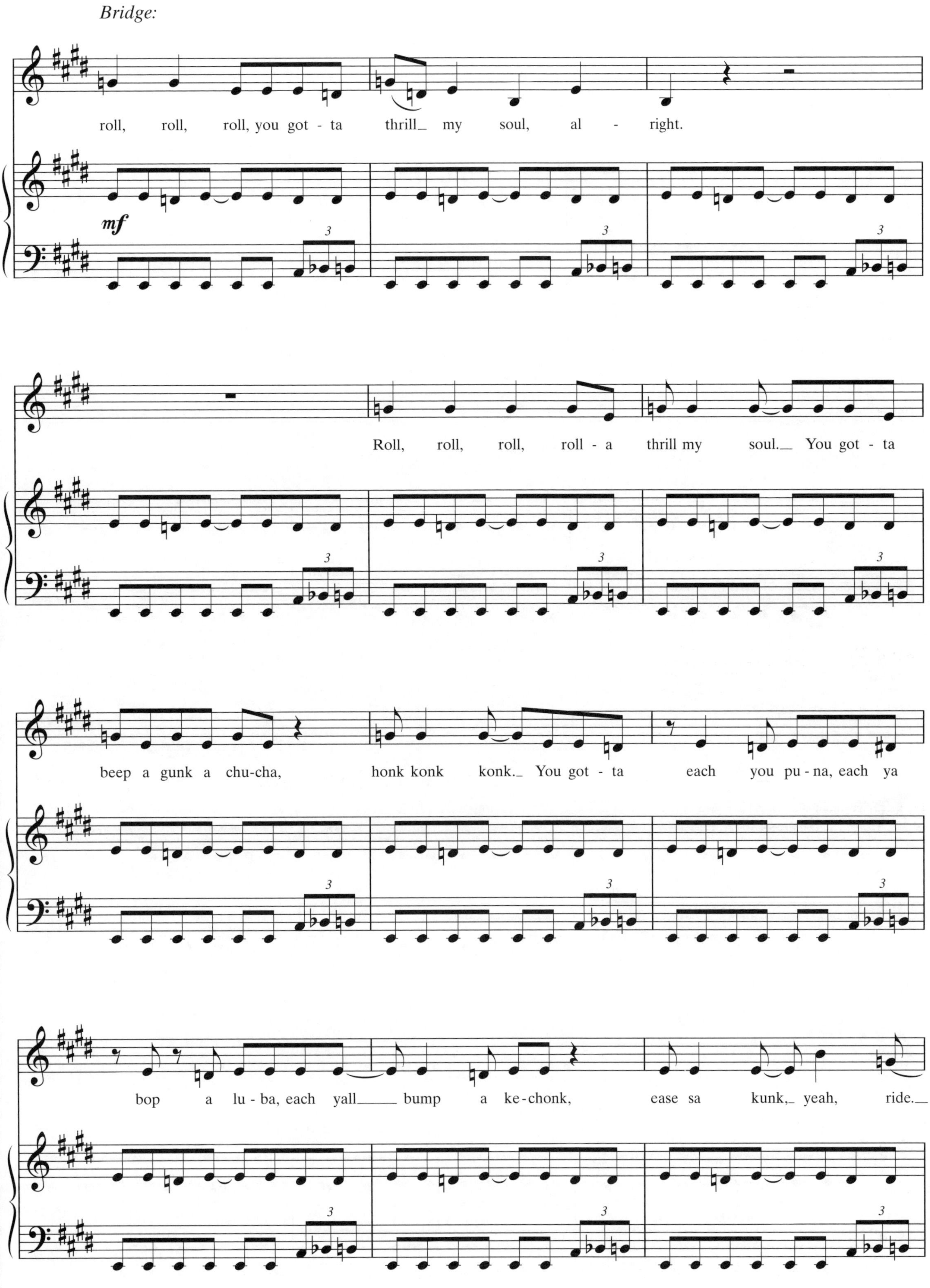
Bridge:
mf
roll, roll, roll, you got - ta thrill_ my soul, al - right.
Roll, roll, roll, roll - a thrill my soul._ You got - ta
beep a gunk a chu-cha, honk konk konk._ You got - ta each you pu - na, each ya
bop a lu - ba, each yall___ bump a ke-chonk, ease sa kunk,_ yeah, ride._

Ash - en la - dy,
ash - en la - dy,
give up your vows,
give up your vows.

Save our cit - y,
save our cit - y,
right now.
3. And, I
Verse 3:
woke up this morn - ing, I got my - self a beer.

And, I
woke up this morn - ing and I got my - self a beer.
The fu-ture's un - cer-tain and the end is al - ways
near.
Let it

Chorus:
A7
roll, ba - by, roll. Let it roll, ba - by, roll.
Let it roll, ba - by, roll.
8va
(8va)
B7
Let it roll,
C7
C♯7
D7
E♭7
E7
N.C.
E9
yeah, all night long.
(8va)

TOUCH ME

Words and Music by
THE DOORS

Moderately ♩ = 116

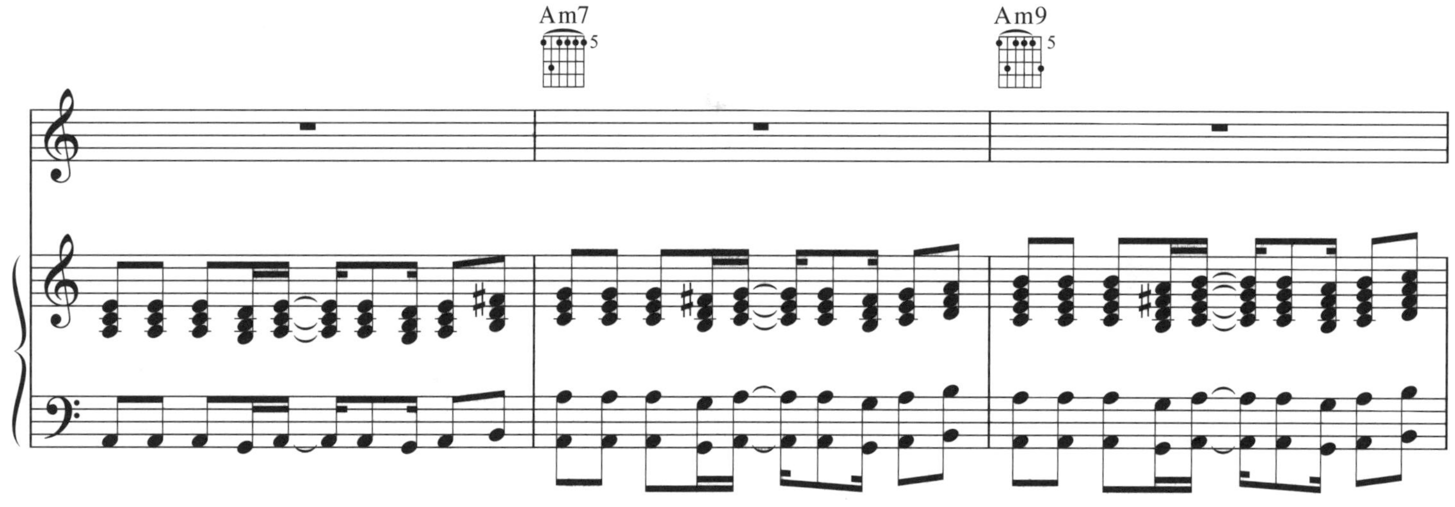

Verse:
G
Bm
C
(1.2.) touch me, babe._ Can't you see that I am not a - fraid._
mf
E♭
B♭
What was that prom - ise that you made?_
Dm
E♭
Why won't you tell me what she_____ said?
G♭
D♭
What was that prom - ise that you made?_

Chorus:
G♭
Fm
Now I'm gon-na love you 'til the
G♭
A♭
D♭
G♭
heav-ens stop the rain. I'm gon - na
Fm
G♭
A♭
G♭
love__ you__ 'til the stars fall__ from the sky for you and
D♭
To Coda
Am
I.
mp

Am7
cresc. poco a poco
Am9
D.S. 𝄋 al Coda
2. Come on, come on, come on, come on now
𝄌 Coda
G♭
Fm
G♭
A♭
I'm gon-na love you 'til the heav-ens stop the
mp
D♭
G♭
Fm
rain. I'm gon-na love you 'til the

G♭
A♭
G♭
D♭
stars fall from the sky for you and I.
mf
Sax solo:
Am
mp
cresc.
Am7
mf
Play 7 times
Am9
f
G
Am